# The Famous Missions of California

BY

W. H. Hudson

# Of Junipero Serra And the Proposed Settlement of Alta California

On the 1st of July, 1769 a day forever memorable in the annals of California—a small party of men, worn out by the fatigues and hardships of their long and perilous journey from San Fernandez de Villicata, came in sight of the beautiful Bay of San Diego. They formed the last division of a tripartite expedition which had for its object the political and spiritual conquest of the great Northwest coast of the Pacific and among their number were Gaspar de Portola, the colonial governor and military commander of the enterprise and Father Junipero Serra, with whose name and achievements the early history of California is indissolubly bound up.

This expedition was the outcome of a determination on the part of Spain to occupy and settle the upper of its California provinces, or Alta California, as it was then called, and thus effectively prevent the more than possible encroachments of the Russians and the English. Fully alive to the necessity of immediate and decisive action, Carlos I. had sent Jose de Galvez out to New Spain, giving him at once large powers as *visitador general* of the provinces, and special instructions to establish military posts at San Diego and Monterey. Galvez was a man of remarkable zeal, energy, and organizing ability, and after the manner of his age and church he regarded his undertaking as equally important from the religious and from the political side. The twofold purpose of his expedition was, as he himself stated it, "to establish the Catholic faith among a numerous heathen people, submerged in the obscure darkness of paganism, and to extend the dominion of the King, our Lord, and protect this peninsula from the ambitious views of foreign nations." From the first it was his intention that the Cross and the flag of Spain should be carried side by side in the task of dominating and colonizing the new country. Having, therefore, gathered his forces together at Santa Ana, near La Paz, he sent thence to Loreto, inviting Junipero Serra, the recently appointed President of the California Missions, to visit him in his camp. Loreto was a hundred leagues distant; but this was no obstacle to the religious enthusiast, whose lifelong dream it had been to bear the faith far and wide among the barbarian peoples of the Spanish world. He hastened to La Paz, and in the course of a long interview with Galvez not only promised his hearty co-operation, but also gave great help in the arrangement of the preliminary details of the expedition.

In the opportunity thus offered him for the missionary labour in hitherto unbroken fields, Father Junipero saw a special manifestation both of the will and of the favour of God. He threw himself into the work with characteristic ardour and determination, and Galvez quickly realized that his own efforts were now to be ably seconded by a man who, by reason of his devotion, courage, and personal magnetism, might well seem to have been providentially designated for the task which had been put into his hands.

Miguel Joseph Serra, now known only by his adopted name of Junipero, which he took out of reverence for the chosen companion of St. Francis, was a native of the Island of Majorca, where he was born, of humble folk, in 1713. According to the testimony of his intimate friend and biographer, Father Francesco Palou, his desires, even during boyhood, were turned towards the religious life. Before he was seventeen he entered the Franciscan Order, a regular member of which he became a year or so later. His favorite reading during his novitiate, Palou tells us, was in the Lives of the Saints, over which he would pore day after day with passionate and ever-growing enthusiasm; and from these devout studies sprang an intense ambition to "imitate the holy and venerable men" who had given themselves up to the grand work of carrying the Gospel among gentiles and savages. The missionary idea thus implanted became the dominant purpose of his life, and neither the astonishing success of his sermons, nor the applause with which his lectures were received when he was made professor of theology, sufficed to dampen his apostolic zeal. Whatever work was given him to do, he did with all his heart, and with all his might, for such was the man's nature; but everywhere and always he looked forward to the mission field as his ultimate career. He was destined, however, to wait many years before his chance came. At length, in 1749, after making many vain petitions to be set apart for foreign service, he and Palou were offered places in a body of priests who, at the urgent request of the College of San Fernando, in Mexico, were then being sent out as recruits to various parts of the New World. The hour had come and in a spirit of gratitude and joy too deep for words, Junipero Serra set his face towards the far lands which were henceforth to be his home.

The voyage out was long and trying. In the first stage of it—from Majorca to Malaga—the dangers and difficulties of seafaring were varied, if not relieved by strange experiences, of which Palou has left us a quaint and graphic account.

Their vessel was a small English coaster, in command of a stubborn cross-patch of a captain, who combined navigation with theology, and whose violent protestations and fondness for doctrinal dispute allowed his Catholic passengers, during the fifteen days of their passage, scarcely a Minute's peace. His habit was to declaim chosen texts out of his "greasy old" English Bible, putting his own interpretation upon them; then, if when challenged by Father Junipero, who "was well trained in dogmatic theology," he could find no verse to fit his argument, he would roundly declare that the leaf he wanted happened to be torn. Such methods are hardly praiseworthy. But this was not the worst. Sometimes the heat of argument would prove too much for him, and then, I grieve to say, he would even threaten to pitch his antagonists overboard, and shape his course for London. However, despite this unlooked-for danger, Junipero and his companions finally reached Malaga, whence they proceeded first to Cadiz, and then, after some delay, to Vera Cruz. The voyage across from Cadiz alone occupied ninety-nine days, though of these, fifteen were spent at Porto Rico, where Father Junipero improved the time by establishing a mission. Hardships were not lacking; for water and food ran short, and the vessel encountered terrific storms. But "remembering the end for which they had come," the father "felt no fear," and his own buoyancy did much to keep up the flagging spirits of those about him. Even when Vera Cruz was reached, the terrible journey was by no means over, for a hundred Spanish leagues lay between that port and the City of Mexico. Too impatient to wait for the animals and wagons which had been promised for transportation, but which, through some oversight or blunder, had not yet arrived in Vera Cruz, Junipero set out to cover the distance on foot. The strain brought on an ulcer in one of his legs, from which he suffered all the rest of his life; and it is highly probable that he would have died on the road but for the quite unexpected succor which came to him more than once in the critical hour. This, according to his wont, he did not fail to refer directly to the special favour of the Virgin and St. Joseph.

For nearly nineteen years after his arrival in Mexico, Junipero was engaged in active missionary work, mainly among the Indians of the Sierra Gorda, whom he successfully instructed in the first principles of the Catholic faith and in the simpler arts of peace. Then came his selection as general head, or president, of the Missions of California, the charge of which, on the expulsion of the Jesuits, in 1768, had passed over to the Franciscans. These, thirteen in number, were all in Lower California, for no attempt had as yet been made to evangelize the upper province. This, however, the indefatigable apostle was now to undertake by co-operating with Jose de Galvez in his proposed northwest expedition. Junipero was now fifty-five years of age, and could look back upon a career of effort and accomplishment which to any less active man might well seem to have earned repose for body and mind. Yet great as his services to church and civilization had been in the past, by far the most important part of his life-work still lay *before him*.

## How Father Junipero Came To San Diego

As a result expedition the should be sent conference out in between two Galvez and Father Junipero, it was decided that their joint expedition should be sent out in two portions—one by sea and one by land; the land portion being again sub-divided into two, in imitation, Palou informs us, of the policy of the patriarch Joseph, "so that if one came to misfortune, the other might still be saved." It was arranged that four missionaries should go into the ships, and one with the advance-detachment of the land-force, the second part of which was to include the president himself. So far as the work of the missionaries was concerned their immediate purpose was to establish three settlements—one at San Diego, a second at Monterey, and a third on a site to be selected, about midway between the two, which was to be called San Buenaventura. The two divisions of the land-force were under the leadership of Captain Fernando Rivera y Moncada and Governor Portola respectively. The ships were to carry all the heavier portions of the camp equipage, provisions, household goods, vestments and sacred vessels; the land-parties were to take with them herds and flocks from Loreto. The understanding was that whichever party first reached San Diego was to wait there twenty days for the rest, and in the event of their failure to arrive within that time, to push on to Monterey.

The sea-detachment of the general expedition—the "Seraphic and Apostolic Squadron," as Palou calls it, was composed o three ships—the *San Carlos*, the *San Antonio*, and the *San Joseph*. A list, fortunately preserved, gives all the persons on board the *San Carlos*, a vessel of about 200 tons only, and the flagship of Don Vicente Vila, the commander of the marine division. They were as follows:—the commander himself; a lieutenant in charge of a company of soldiers; a missionary; the captain, pilot and surgeon; twenty-five soldiers; the officers and crew of the ship, twenty-five in all; the baker, the cook and two assistants; and two blacksmiths: total, sixty-two souls. An inventory shows that the vessel was provisioned for eight months.

The *San Carlos* left La Paz on the 9th of January; the *San Antonio* on the 15th of February; the *San Joseph* on the 16th of June. All the vessels met with heavy storms, and the *San Carlos*, being driven sadly out of her route, did not reach San Diego till twenty days after the *San Antonio*, though dispatched some five weeks earlier. We shudder to read that of her crew but one sailor and the cook were left alive; the rest, along with many of the soldiers, having succumbed to the scurvy. The San Antonio also lost eight of her crew from the same dreadful disease. These little details serve better than any general description to give us an idea of the horrible conditions of Spanish seamanship in the middle of the eighteenth century. As for the *San Joseph*, she never reached her destination at all, though where and how she met her fate remains one of the dark mysteries of the ocean. Two small points in connection with her loss are perhaps sufficiently curious to merit notice. In the first place, she was the only one of the ships that had no missionary on board; and secondly, she was called after the very saint who had been named special patron of the entire undertaking.

The original plan, as we have seen, had been that Father Junipero should accompany the governor in the second division of the land-expedition; but this, when the day fixed for departure came, was found to be quite impossible owing to the ulcerous sore on his leg, which had been much aggravated by the exertions of his recent hurried journey from Loreto to La Paz and back. Greatly chafing under the delay, he was none the less obliged to postpone his start for several weeks. At length, on the 28th of March, in company with two soldiers and a servant, he mounted his mule and set out. The event showed that he had been guilty of undue haste, for he suffered terribly on the rough way, and on reaching San Xavier, whither he went to turn over the management of the Lower California missions to Palou, who was then settled there, his condition was such that his friend implored him to remain behind, and allow him (Palau) to go forward in his stead. But of this Junipero would not hear, for he regarded himself as specially chosen and called by God for the work to which he stood, body and soul, committed. "Let us speak no more of this," he said. "I have placed all my faith in God, through whose goodness I hope to reach not only San Diego, to plant and fix there the standard of the Holy Cross, but even as far as Monterey." And Palou, seeing that Junipero was not to be turned aside, wisely began to talk of other things.

After three days devoted to business connected with the missions of the lower province, the indomitable father determined to continue his journey, notwithstanding the fact that, still totally unable to move his leg, he had to be lifted by two men into the saddle. We may imagine that poor Palou found it hard enough to answer his friend's cheery farewells, and watched him with sickness of heart as he rode slowly away. It seemed little likely indeed that they would ever meet again on this side of the grave. But Junipero's courage never gave out. Partly for rest and partly for conference with those in charge, he lingered awhile at the missions along the way; but, nevertheless, presently came up with Portola and his detachment, with whom he proceeded to Villicata. Herd during a temporary halt, lie founded a mission which was dedicated to San Fernando, King of Castile and Leon. But the worst experiences of the journey were still in store. For when the party was ready to move forward again towards San Diego, which, as time was fast running on, the commander was anxious to reach with the least possible delay, it was found that Junipero's leg was in such an inflamed condition that he could neither stand, nor sit, nor sleep. For a few leagues he persevered, without complaint to any one, and then collapsed. Portola urged him to return at once to San Fernando for the complete repose in which alone there seemed any chance of recovery, but after his manner Junipero refused; nor, out of kindly feeling for the tired native servants, would he ever hear of the litter which the commander thereupon proposed to have constructed for his transportation. The situation was apparently beyond relief, when, after prayer to God, the padre called to him one of the muleteers. "Son," he said—the conversation is reported in full by Palou, from whose memoir of his friend it is here translated—"do you not know how to make a remedy for the ulcer on my foot and leg?" And the muleteer replied: "Father, how should I know of any remedy? Am I a surgeon, I am a mule-driver, and can only cure harness-wounds on animals." "Then, son," rejoined Junipero, "consider that I am an animal, and that this ulcer is a harness-wound . . . and prepare for me the same medicament as you would make for a beast." Those who heard this request smiled. And the muleteer obeyed; and mixing certain herbs with hot tallow, applied the compound to the ulcerated leg, with the astonishing result that the sufferer slept that night in absolute comfort, and was perfectly able the next morning to undertake afresh the fatigues of the road.

Of the further incidents of the tedious journey it is needless to write. It is enough to say that for forty-six days—from the 15th of May to the 1st of July—the little party plodded on, following the track of the advance-division of the land-expedition under Rivera y Moncada. With what joy and gratitude they at last looked down upon the harbour of San Diego, and realized that the first object of their efforts had now indeed been achieved, may be readily imagined. Out in the bay lay the *San Carlos* and the *San Antonio*, and on the shore were the tents of the men who had preceded them, and of whose safety they were now assured; and when, with volley after volley, they announced their arrival, ships and camp replied in glad salute. And this responsive firing was continued, says Palou, in his lively description of the scene, "until, all having alighted, they were ready to testify their mutual love by close embraces and affectionate rejoicing to see the, expeditions thus joined, and at their desired destination." Yet one cannot but surmise that the delights of reunion were presently chilled when those who had thus been spared to come together fell into talk over the companions who had perished by the way. History has little to tell us of such details; but the sympathetic reader will hardly fail to provide them for himself.

The condition of things which the governor and the president and confronting them on their arrival was indeed the reverse of satisfactory. Of the one hundred and thirty or so men comprising the combined companies, many were seriously ill; some it was necessary to dispatch at once with the *San Antonio* back to San Blas for additional supplies and reinforcements; a further number had to be detailed for the expedition to Monterey, which, in accordance with the explicit instructions of the visitador general it was decided to send out immediately. All this left the San Diego camp extremely short-handed, but there was no help for it. To reach Monterey at all costs was Portola's' next duty; and on the 14th of July, with a small party which included Fathers Crespi and Gomez, he commenced its northwest march.

## OF THE FOUNDING OF THE MISSION AT SAN DIEGO

In the meanwhile, says Palou, "that fervent zeal which continually glowed and burned in the heart of our venerable Father Junipero, did not permit him o forget the principal object of his journey." A soon as Portola had left the encampment, he began to busy himself with the problem of the mission which, it had been determined, should be founded on that spot. Ground was carefully chosen with an eye to the requirements, not only of the mission itself, but also of the *pueblo*, or village, which in course of time would almost certainly grow up about it; and on the 16th of July—the day upon which, as the anniversary of a great victory over the Moors in 1212, the Spanish church solemnly celebrated the Triumph of the Holy Cross—the first mission of Upper California was dedicated to San Diego de Alcali, after whom the bay had been named by Sebastian Viscaino, the explorer, many years before. The ceremonies were a repetition of those which had been employed in the founding of the Mission of San Fernando at Villicata; the site was blessed and sprinkled with holy water; a great cross reared, facing the harbour; the mass celebrated; the *Venite Creator Spiritus* sung. And, as before, where the proper accessories failed, Father Junipero and his colleagues fell back undeterred upon the means which Heaven had actually put at their disposal. The constant firing of the troops supplied the lack of musical instruments, and the smoke of the powder was accepted as a substitute for incense. Father Palou's brief and unadorned description will not prove altogether wanting in impressiveness for those who in imagination can conjure up a picture of the curious, yet dramatic scene.

The preliminary work of foundation thus accomplished, Father Junipero gathered about him the few healthy men who could be spared from the tending of their sick comrades and routine duties, and with their help erected a few rude huts, one of which was immediately consecrated as a temporary chapel. So far as his own people were concerned, the *padre's* labours were for the most part of a grievous character, for, during the first few months, the records tell us, disease made such fearful ravages among the soldiers, sailors and servants, that ere long the number of persons at this settlement had been reduced to twenty. But the tragedy of these poor nameless fellows—(it was Junipero's pious hope that they might all be named in Heaven)—after all hardly forms part of our proper story. The father's real work was to lie among the native Indians, and it is with his failures and successes in this direction that the main interest of our California mission annals is connected.

They were not an attractive people, these "gentiles" of a country which to the newcomers must itself have seemed an outer garden of Paradise; and Junipero's first attempts to gain their good will met with very slight encouragement. During the ceremonies attendant upon the foundation and dedication of the mission, they had stood round in silent wonder, and now they showed themselves responsive to the strangers' advances to the extent of receiving whatever presents were offered, provided the gift was not in the form of anything to eat. The Spaniards' food they would not even touch, apparently regarding it as the cause of the dire sickness of the troops. And this, in the long run, remarks Palou, was without doubt "singularly providential," owing to the rapid depletion of the stores. Ignorance of the Indians' language, of course, added seriously to the father's difficulties in approaching them, and presently their thefts of cloth, for the possession of which they developed a perfect passion, and other depredations, rendered them exceedingly troublesome. Acts of violence became more and more common, and by-and-bye, a determined and organized attack upon the mission, in which the assailants may times outnumbered their opponents, led to a pitched battle, and the death of one of the Spanish servants. This was the crisis, for, happily, like a thunderstorm, the disturbance, which seemed so threatening of future cleared the air, at any rate for a time; and the kindness with which the Spaniards treated their wounded foes evidently touched the savage heart.

Little by little a few Indians here and there began to frequent the mission; and with the hearty welcome accorded them their numbers soon increased. Among them there happened to be a boy, of some fifteen years of age, who showed himself more tractable than his fellows, and whom Father Junipero determined to use as an instrument for his purpose. When the lad had picked up a smattering of Spanish, the padre sent him to his people with the promise that if he were allowed to bring back one of the children, the youngster should not only by baptism be made a Christian, but should also (and here the good father descended to a bribe) be tricked out like the Spaniards themselves, in handsome clothes. A few days later, a "gentile," followed by a large crowd, appeared with a child n his arms, and the *padre*, filled with unutterable joy, at once threw a piece of cloth over and called upon one of the soldiers to stand godfather to this first infant of Christ. But, alas just as he was preparing to sprinkle the holy water, the natives snatched the child from him, and made off with it (and the cloth) to their own rancheria. The soldiers who stood round as witnesses were furious at this insult, and, left to themselves, would have inflicted summary punishment upon the offenders. But the good father pacified them, attributing his failure—of which he was wont to speak tearfully to the end of his life—to his own sins and unworthiness. However, this first experience in convert-making was fortunately not prophetic, for though it is true that many months elapsed before a single neophyte was gained for the mission, and though more serious troubles were still to come, in the course of the next few years a number of the aborigines, both children and adults, were baptized.

## Of Portola's Quest for the Harbor of Monterey and the Founding of the Mission of San Carlos

While Junipero and his companions were thus engaged in planting the faith among the Indians of San Diego, Portola's expedition was meeting with unexpected trials and disappointments. The harbour of Monterey had been discovered and described by Viscaino at the beginning of the seventeenth century, and it seemed no very difficult matter to reach it by way of the coast. But either the charts misled them, or their own calculations erred, or the appearance of the landscape was strangely deceptive. At any rate, for whatever reason or combination of reasons, the exploring party passed the harbour without recognizing it, though actually lingering awhile on the sand hills overlooking the bay. Half persuaded in their bewilderment that some great catastrophe must, since Viscaino's observations, have obliterated the port altogether, they pressed northward another forty leagues, and little dreaming of the importance attaching to their wanderings, crossed the Coast range, and looked down thence over the Santa Clara valley and the "immense arm" of San Francisco Bay. By this time the rainy season had set in, and convinced as they now were that they must, through some oversight or ill-chance, have missed the object of their quest, they determined to retrace their steps, and institute another and more thorough search. On again reaching the neighborhood of Monterey, they spent a whole fortnight in systematic exploration, but still, strangely enough, without discovering "any indication or landmark" of the harbour. Baffled and disheartened, therefore, the leaders resolved to abandon the enterprise. They then erected two large wooden crosses as memorials of their visit, and cutting on one of these the word "Dig at the foot of this and you will find a writing"—buried there a brief narrative of their experiences. This is reproduced in the diary of Father Crespi; and its closing words have a touch of simple pathos:—"At last, undeceived, and despairing of finding it [the harbour] after so many efforts, sufferings and labours, and having left of all our provisions but fourteen small sacks of flour, our expedition leaves this place to-day for San Diego; I beg of Almighty God to guide it, and for thee, voyager, that His divine providence may lead thee to the harbour of salvation. Done in this Bay of Pinos, the 9th of December, 1769." On the cross on the other side of Point Pinos was cut with a razor this legend:—"The land expedition returned to San Diego for want of provisions, this 9th day of December, 1769."

The little party—or more correctly speaking—what was left bf it, did not reach San Diego till the 25th of the following month, having in their march down suffered terribly from hunger, exposure, wet, fatigue and sickness. Depressed themselves, they found nothing to encourage them in the mission and camp, where death had played havoc among those they had left behind them six months before, and where the provisions were so fast running low that only the timely reappearance of the *San Antonio*, long overdue, would save the survivors from actual starvation. Perhaps it is hardly surprising that, under these circumstances, Portola's courage should have failed him, and that he should have decided upon a return to Mexico. He caused an inventory of all available provisions to be taken, and calculating that, with strict economy, and setting aside what would be required for the journey back to San Fernando, they might last till somewhat beyond the middle of March, he gave out that unless the *San Antonio* should arrive by the loth of that month, he should on that day abandon San Diego, and start south. But if the governor imagined for a moment that he could persuade the *padre presidente* to fall in with this arrangement, he did not know his man. Junipero firmly believed, despite the failure of Portola's expedition, that the harbour of Monterey still existed, and might be found; he even interested Vicente Vila in a plan of his own for reaching it by sea; and he furthermore made up his mind that, come what might, nothing should ever induce him to turn his back upon his work.

Then a wonderful thing happened. On the 19th of March—the very day before that fixed by the governor for his departure, and when everything was in readiness for tomorrow's march—the sail of a ship appeared far out at sea; and though the vessel presently disappeared towards the northwest, it returned four days later and proved to be one other than the *San Antonio*, bearing the much needed succour. She had passed up towards Monterey in the expectation of finding the larger body of settlers there, and had only put back to San Diego when unexpectedly, (and as it seemed, providentially), she had run short of water. It was inevitable that Father Junipero should see in this series of happenings the very hand of God—the more so as the day of relief chanced to be the festival of St. Joseph, who, as we have noted, was the patron of the mission enterprise.

The arrival of the *San Antonio* put an entirely new complexion upon affairs; and, relieved of immediate anxiety,

Portola now resolved upon a second expedition in quest o Monterey. Two divisions, one for sea, the other for land, were accordingly made ready; the former, which included Junipero, started in the *San Antonio*, on the 16th of April; the latter, under the leadership of Portola, a day later. Strong adverse winds interfered with the vessel, which did not make Monterey for a month and a half. The land-party, following the coast, reached the more southern of the great wooden crosses on the 24th of May, and after some difficulty succeeded at last in identifying the harbour. Seven days later, steering by the fires lighted for her guidance along the shore, the *San Antonio* came safely into port; and formal possession of the bay and surrounding country was presently taken in the name of church and King.

This was on the 3rd of June, the Feast of Pentecost; and on that day of peculiar significance in the apostolic history of the church, the second of the Upper California missions came into being. Palou has left us a full account of the ceremonies. Governor, soldiers and priests gathered together on the beach, on the spot where in 1603, the Carmelite fathers who had accompanied Viscaino, had celebrated the mass. An altar was improvised and bells rung; and then, in alb and stole, the father-president invoked the aid of the Holy Ghost, solemnly chanted the *Venite Creator Spiritus;* blessed and raised a great cross; "to put to flight all the infernal enemies;" and sprinkled with holy water the beach and adjoining fields. Mass was then sung; Father Junipero preached a sermon again the roar of cannon and muskets took the place of instrumental music; and the function was concluded with the *Te Deum*. Though now commonly called Carmelo, or Carmel, from the river across which it looks, and which has thus lent it a memory of the first Christian explorers on the spot, this mission is properly known by the name of San Carlos Borromeo, Cardinal-Archbishop of Milan. A few huts enclosed by a palisade, and forming the germ at once of the religious and of the military settlement, were hastily erected. But the actual building of the mission was not begun until the summer of 1771.

# How Father Junipero Established the Missions Of San Antonio De Padua, San Gabriel, and San Louis Obispo

News of the establishment of the missions and military posts at San Diego and Monterey was in due course carried to the City of Mexico, where it so delighted the Marques de Croix, Viceroy of New Spain, and Jose de Galvez, that they not only set the church bells ringing, but forthwith began to make arrangements for the founding of more missions in the upper province. Additional priests were provided by the College of San Fernando; funds liberally subscribed; and the *San Antonio* made ready to sail from San Blas with the friars and supplies. On the 21st of May, 1771, the good ship dropped anchor at Monterey, where, in the meantime, Junipero, though busy enough among the natives of the neighborhood, was suffering grievous disappointment because, from lack of priests and soldiers, he was unable to proceed at once with the proposed establishment of San Buenaventura. The safe arrival of ten assistants now brought him assurance of a rapid extension of work in "the vineyard of the Lord." He was not the man to let time slip by him unimproved. Plans were immediately laid for carrying the cross still further into the wilderness, and six new missions—those of San Buenaventura, San Gabriel, San Louis Obispo, San Antonio, Santa Clara and San Francisco—were presently agreed upon. It was discovered later on, however, that these plans outran the resources at the president's disposal, and much to his regret, the design for settlements at Santa Clara and San Francisco had to be temporarily given up.

There was, none the less, plenty to engage the energies of even so tireless a worker as Junipero, for three of the new missions were successfully established between July, 1771, and the autumn of the following year. The first of these was the Mission of San Antonio de Padua, in a beautiful spot among the Santa Lucia mountains, some twenty-five leagues southeast of Monterey the second, that of San Gabriel Archangel, near what is now known as the San Gabriel river; and the third, the Mission of San Luis Obispo de Tolosa, for which a location was chosen near the coast, about twenty-five leagues southeast of San Antonio.

In his account of the founding of the first named of these, Palou throws in a characteristic touch. After the bells had been hung on trees and loudly tolled, he says, the excited *padre-presidente* began to shout like one transported:—"Ho, gentiles! Come to the Holy Church; Come! Come and receive the faith of Jesus Christ!" His comrade, Father Pieras, standing by astonished, interrupted his fervent eloquence with the eminently practical remark that as there were no gentiles within hearing, it was idle to ring the bells. But the enthusiast's ardour was not to be damped by such considerations, and he continued to ring and shout. I, for one, am grateful for such a detail as this.

An even more significant story, though of a quite different sort, is recorded of the dedication of San Gabriel. It was, of course, inevitable that here and there in connection with such a record as this of Serra and his work, there should spring up legends of miraculous doings and occurrences; though on the whole, it is, perhaps, remarkable that the mythopoeic tendency was not more powerful. The incident now referred to may be taken as an illustration. While the missionary party were engaged in exploring for a suitable site, a large force of natives, under two chiefs, suddenly broke in upon them. Serious conflict seemed imminent; when one of the fathers drew forth a piece of canvas bearing the picture of the Virgin. Instantly the savages threw their weapons to the ground, and, following their leaders, crowded with offerings about the marvellous image. Thus the danger was averted. Further troubles attended the settlement at San Gabriel but in after years it became one of the most successful of all the missions, and gained particular fame from the industries maintained by its converts, and their skill in carving wood, horn and leather.

# Of the Tragedy at San Diego and Missions at San Juan Capistrano, San Francisco, Santa Clara

Though, as we thus see, Father Junipero had ample reason to be encouraged over the progress of his enterprise, he still had various difficulties to contend with. The question of supplies often assumed formidable proportions, and the labors of the missionaries were not always as fruitful as had been hoped. Fortunately, however, the Indians were, as a rule, friendly, notwithstanding the fact that the behaviour of the Spanish soldiers, especially towards their women, occasionally aroused their distrust and resentment. At one establishment only did serious disturbances actually threaten for a time the continuance of the mission and its work. Junipero had lately returned from Mexico, with undiminished zeal and all sorts of fresh designs revolving in his brain, when a courier reached him at San Carlos bringing news of a terrible disaster at San Diego. Important affairs detained him for a time at Monterey, but when at length he was able to get to the scene of the trouble, it was to find that first reports had not been exaggerated. On the night of the 4th of November, 1775, eight hundred Indians had made a ferocious assault upon the mission, fired the buildings, and brutally done to death Father Jayme, one of the two priests in charge. "God be thanked," Junipero had exclaimed, when the letter containing the dreadful news had been read to him, "now the soil is watered, and the conquest of the Dieguinos will soon be complete!" In the faith that the blood of the martyrs is veritably the seed of the church, he, on reaching San Diego, with his customary energy, set about the task of re-establishing the mission; and the buildings which presently arose from the ruins were a great improvement upon those which had been destroyed.

Before these alarming events at the mother-mission broke in upon his regular work, the president had resolved upon yet another settlement (not included in the still uncompleted plan), for which he had selected a point on the coast some twenty-six leagues north of San Diego, and which was to be dedicated to San Juan Capistrano. A beginning had indeed been made there, not by Junipero in person, but by fathers delegated by him to the purpose; but when news of the murder of Father Jayme reached them, they had hastily buried bells, chasubles and supplies, and hurried south. As soon as ever he felt it wise to leave San Diego Junipero himself now repaired to the abandoned site; and there, on the 1st of November, 1776, the bells were dug up and hung, mass said, and the mission established. It is curious to remember that while the *padre-presidente* was thus immersed in apostolic labors on the far Pacific coast, on the other side of the North American continent events of a very different character were shaking the whole civilized world.

Though the establishment of San an Capistrano is naturally mentioned in this place, partly because of the abortive start made there a year before, and partly because its actual foundation constituted the next noteworthy incident in Junipero's career, this mission is, in strict chronological order, not the sixth, but the seventh on our list. For some three weeks before its dedication, and without the knowledge of the president himself, though in full accordance with his designs, the cross had been planted at a point many leagues northward beyond San Carlos, and destined presently to be the most important on the coast. It will be remembered that when Portola's party made their first futile search for the harbour of Monterey, they had by accident found their way as far as the Bay of San Francisco. The significance of their discovery was not appreciated at the time, either by themselves or by those at headquarters to whom it was reported; but later explorations so clearly established the value of the spot for settlement and fortification, that it was determined to build a presidio there. Some years previous to this, as we have seen, a mission on the northern bay had been part of Junipero's ambitious scheme; and though at the time he was forced by circumstances to hold his hand, the idea was constantly uppermost in his thoughts. At length, when, in the summer of 1776, an expedition was despatched from Monterey for the founding of the proposed presidio, two missionaries were included in the party—one of these being none other than that Father Palou, whose records have been our chief guides in the course of this story. The buildings of the presidio—store house, commandant's dwelling, and huts for the soldiers and their families—were completed by the middle of September; and on the 17th of that month—the day of St. Francis, patron of the station and harbour—imposing ceremonies of foundation were performed. A wooden church was then built; and on the 9th of October, in the presence of many witnesses, Father Palou said mass, the image of St. Francis was borne about in procession, and the mission solemnly dedicated to his name.

It was at San is Obispo on his way back from San Diego to Monterey, that Father Junipero learned of the foundation of the mission at San Francisco, and though he may doubtless have felt some little regret at not having himself been present on such an occasion, his heart overflowed with joy. For there was a special reason why the long delay in carrying out this portion of his plan had weighed heavily upon him. Years before, when the *visitador general* had told him that the first three missions in Alta California were to be named after San Diego, San Carlos and San Buenaventura (for such, we recollect, had been the original programme), he had exclaimed:—"Then is our father, St. Francis, to have no mission?" And Galvez had made reply:—"If St. Francis desires a mission, let him show us his port, and he shall have one there." To Junipero it had seemed that Portola had providentially been led beyond Monterey to the Bay of San Francisco, and the founder of his order had thus given emphatic answer to the *visitador's* words. It may well be imagined that he was ill at rest until the saint's wishes had been earned into effect.

But this was not the only good work done in the north while Junipero was busy elsewhere; for on the 12th of January, 1777, the Mission of Santa Clara was established in the wonderfully fertile and beautiful valley which is now known by that name. The customary rites were performed by Father Tomas de la Pella, a rude chapel erected, and the work of constructing the necessary buildings of the settlement immediately begun.

It should be noted in passing that before the end of the year the town of San Jose—or, to give it its full Spanish title, El Pueblo de San Jose de Guadalupe was founded near by. This has historic interest as the first purely civil settlement in California. The fine Alameda from the mission to the pueblo was afterwards made and laid out under the fathers' supervision.

# Of the Mission of San Buenaventura, and of the Death and Character of Father Junipero.

Though Junipero's subordinates had thus done without him in these important developments at San Francisco and Santa Clara, he still resolved to go north, both to visit the new foundations and to inspect for himself the marvellous country of which he had heard much, but which he had not yet seen. As usual, he was long detained by urgent affairs, and it was not till autumn that he succeeded in breaking away. He made a short stay at Santa Clara, and then pushed on to San Francisco, which he reached in time to say mass on St. Francis' day. After a ten days' rest, he crossed to the presidio and feasted his eyes on the glorious vision of the Golden Gate—a sight which once seen is never to be forgotten. "Thanks be to God!" he cried, in rapture (these, says Palou, were the words most frequently on his lips); "now our Father St. Francis, with the Holy Cross of the procession of missions, has reached the ultimate end of this continent of California. To go further ships will be required!" Yet his joy was tempered with the thought that the eight missions already founded were very far apart, and that much labour would be necessary to fill up the gaps.

It was thus with the feeling that, while something had been done, far more was left to do, that the padre returned to his own special charge at San Carlos. Various circumstances in combination had caused the postponement, year after year, of that third mission, which, according to original intentions, was to have followed immediately upon the establishments at San Diego and Monterey. Three new settlements were now projected on the Santa Barbara Channel, and the first of these was to be the mission of San Buenaventura. It was not until 1782, however, that the long-delayed purpose was at length accomplished. The site chosen was at the southeastern extremity of the channel, and dose to an Indian village, or *rancheria* to which Portola's expedition in 1769 had given the name of *Ascension de Nuestra Senora*, or, briefly, *Assumpta*. A little later on, in pursuance of the same plan, the then governor, Filipe de Neve, took formal possession of a spot some ten leagues distant, and there began the construction of the *presidio* of Santa Barbara. It was Junipero's earnest desire to proceed at once with the adjoining mission. But the governor, for reasons of his own, threw obstacles in the way, and in the end this fresh undertaking was left to other hands.

For we have now come to the close of Father Junipero's long and strenuous career and as we look back over the record of it, our wonder is, not that he should have died when he did, but rather that he had not killed himself many years before. His is surely one of those cases in which supreme spiritual power and sheer force of will triumph over an accumulation of bodily ills. Far from robust of constitution, he had never given himself consideration or repose, forcing himself to exertions which it would have appeared utterly impossible that his frame could bear, and adding to the constant strain of his labours and travels the hardships of self-inflicted tortures of a severe ascetic regime. He had always been much troubled by the old ulcer on his leg, though this, no matter how painful, he never regarded save when it actually incapacitated him for work; and for many years he had suffered from a serious affection of the heart, which had been greatly aggravated, even if it was not in the first instance caused, by his habit of beating himself violently on his chest with a huge stone, at the conclusion of his sermons—to the natural horror of his hearers, who, it is said, were often alarmed lest he should drop dead before their eyes. The fatal issue of such practices could only be a question of time. At length, mental anxiety and sorrow added their weight to his burden—particularly disappointment at the slow progress of his enterprise, and grief over the death of his fellow-countryman and close friend, Father Crespi, who passed to his well-earned rest on New Year's Day, 1782. After this loss, it is recorded, he was never the same man again, though he held so tenaciously to his duties, that only a year before the call came to him, being then over seventy, he limped from San Diego to Monterey, visiting his missions, and weeping over the outlying Indian *rancherias*, because he was powerless to help the unconverted dwellers in them. He died at San Carlos, tenderly nursed to the end by the faithful Palou, on the 28th August, 1784 and his passing was so peaceful that those watching thought him asleep. On hearing the mission bells toll for his death, the whole population, knowing well what had occurred, burst into tears; and when, clothed in the simple habit of his order, his body was laid out in his cell, the native neophytes crowded in with flowers, while the Spanish soldiers and sailors pressed round in the hope of being blessed by momentary contact with his corpse, He was laid beneath the mission altar beside his beloved friend Crespi but when, in after years, a new church was built, the remains of both were removed and placed within it.

It is not altogether easy to measure such a man as Junipero Serra by our ordinary modern standards of character and conduct. He was essentially a religious enthusiast, and as a religious enthusiast he must be judged. To us who read his story from a distance, who breathe an atmosphere totally different from his, and whose lives are governed by quite other passions and ideals, he may often appear one-sided, extravagant, deficient in tact and forethought; and, in the excess of his zeal, too ready to sacrifice everything to the purposes he never for an instant allowed to drop out of his sight. We may even, with some of his critics, protest that was not a man of powerful intellect; that his views of people and things were distressingly narrow that, after his kind, he was extremely superstitious; that he was despotic in his dealings with his converts, and stiff-necked in his relations with the civil and military authorities. For all this is doubtless true. But all this must not prevent us from seeing him as he actually was—charitable, large-hearted, energetic, indomitable; in all respects a remarkable, in many ways, a really wise and great man. At whatever points he may fall short of our criteria, this much must be said of him, that he was fired throughout with the high spirit of his vocation, that he was punctual in the performance of duty as he understood it, that he was obedient to the most rigorous dictates of that Gospel which he had set himself to preach. In absolute, single-hearted, unflinching, and tireless devotion to the task of his life—the salvation of heathen souls—he spent himself freely and cheerfully, a true follower of that noblest and most engaging of the mediaeval saints, whose law he had laid upon himself, and whom he looked up to as his guide and examplar. Let us place him where he belongs—among the transcendent apostolic figures of his own church; for thus alone shall we do justice to his personality, his objects, his career. The memory Of such a man will survive all changes in creeds and ideals;

and the great state, of which he was the first pioneer, will do honour to herself in honoring him.

# How the Missions of Santa Barbara, La Purisima Conception, Santa Cruz, Soledad, San Jose, San Juan Bautista, San Miguel, San Fernando, San Luis Rey, and Santa Inez, Were Added to the List.

After Junipero's death the supervision of the missions devolved for a time upon Palou, under whose management, owing to difficulties with the civil powers, no new foundations were undertaken, though satisfactory progress was made in those already existing. In 1786, Palou was appointed head of the College of San Fernando, and his place as mission president was filled by Father Firmin Francisco de Lasuen, by whom the mission of Santa Barbara was dedicated, on the festival day of that virgin-martyr, before the close of the year. Just twelve months later, the third channel settlement was started, with the performance of the usual rites, on the spot fixed for the Mission of La Purisima Concepcion, at the western extremity of the bay; though some months passed before real work there was begun. Thus the proposed scheme, elaborated before Junipero's death, for the occupation of that portion of the coast, was at length successfully carried out.

Hardly had this been accomplished before the viceroy and governor, having resolved upon a further extension of the mission system, sent orders to Father Lasuen to proceed with two fresh settlements, one of which was to be dedicated to the Holy Cross, the other to Our Lady of Solitude. Time was, as usual, consumed in making the necessary preparations, and the two missions were finally founded within a few weeks of each other—on the 28th of August and the 9th of October, 1791, respectively. The site selected for the Mission of Santa Cruz was in the neighborhood already known by that name, and near the San Lorenzo River; that of Nuestra Senora de la Soledad, on the west side of the Salinas River, in the vicinity of the present town of Soledad, and about thirty miles from Monterey.

A glance at the map of California will help us to understand the policy which had dictated the creation of the four missions founded since Junipero's death. The enormous stretch of country between San Francisco and San Diego, the northern and southern extremes of evangelical enterprise, was as yet quite insufficiently occupied, and these new settlements had been started with the object of to some extent filling up the vast vacant spaces still left among those already existing. For the efficient performance of missionary work something more was needed than a number of separate establishments, no matter how well managed and successful these in them selves might be. Systematic organization was essential for this it was requisite that the various missions should be brought, by proximity, into vital relations with one another, that communication might be kept up, companionship enjoyed, and, in case of need, advice given and assistance rendered. The foundations of Santa Barbara, La Purisima, Santa Cruz and Soledad, had done something, as will be seen, towards the ultimate drawing together of the scattered outposts of church and civilization. But with them a beginning had only been made. Further developments of the same general plan which aimed, it will be understood, not alone at the spiritual conquest, but also at the proper control of the new kingdom—were now taken under consideration. And, as a result, five fresh missions were presently resolved upon. One of these was to be situated between San Francisco and Santa Clara; the second, between Santa Clara and Monterey; the third, between San Antonio and San Luis Obispo; the fourth, between San Buenaventura and San Gabriel; and the fifth, between San Juan Capistrano and San Diego. The importance of these proposed settlements as connecting links will be at once apparent, if we observe that by reason of their carefully chosen locations they served, as it were, to put the older missions into actual touch. When at length the preliminary arrangements had been made, no time was wasted in the carrying out of the programme, and in a little over a year, all five missions were in operation. The mission San Jose (a rather tardy recognition to the patron-saint of the whole undertaking), was founded on the 11th June, 1797; San Juan Bautista thirteen days later; an Miguel Archangel on the 25th July, and San Fernando Rey de Espana on the 8th September of the same year; and San Luis Rey de Francis (commonly called San Luis Rey to distinguish it from San Luis Obispo), on the 13th of the July following. The delay which had not at all been anticipated in the establishment of this last-named mission, was due to some difficulties in regard to site. With this ended—so far as fresh foundations were concerned—the pious labours of Lasuen as *padre-presidente*. He now returned to San Carlos to devote himself during the remainder of his life to the arduous duties of supervision and administration. There he died, in 1803, aged eighty-three years.

His successor, Father Estevan Tapis, fourth president of the Upper California missions, signalized his elevation to office by adding a nineteenth to the establishments under his charge. Founded on the 17th September, 1804, on a spot, eighteen miles from La Purisima and twenty-two from Santa Barbara, on which Lasuen had already directed attention, this was dedicated to the virgin-martyr, Santa Inez. It was felt that a settlement somewhere in this region was still needed for the completion of the mission system, since without it, a gap was left in the line between the two missions first-named, which were some forty miles apart. With the planting of Santa Inez thorough spiritual occupation may be said to have been accomplished over the, entire area between San Francisco and San Diego, and from the Coast Range to the ocean. The nineteen missions had been so distributed over the vast country, that the Indians scattered through it could everywhere be reached; while the distance from mission to mission had at the same time, been so reduced that it was in no case too great to be easily covered in a single day's journey. The fathers of each establishment could thus had frequent intercourse with their next neighbors, and occasional travellers moving to and fro on business could from day to day be certain of finding a place for refreshment and repose.

# Of the Founding of the Missions of San Raphael and San Francisco Solano

Santa Inez carries us for the first time over into the nineteenth century, and its establishment may in a sense be regarded as marking the term of the period of expansion in California mission history. A pause of more than a decade ensued, during which no effort was made towards the further spread of the general system; and then, with the planting of two relatively unimportant settlements in a district thentofore unoccupied the tally was brought to a close.

The missions which thus represented a slight and temporary revival of the old spirit of enterprise, were those of San Rafael Archangel and San Francisco Solano. The former, located near Mount Tamalpais, between San Francisco de Assis and the Russian military station at Fort Ross, dates from the 17th December, 1817; the latter, situated still further north, in the Sonoma Valley, from the 4th July, 1823. Some little uncertainty exists as to the true reasons and purposes of their foundation. The commonly accepted version of the story connects them directly with problems which arose out of the course of affairs at San Francisco. In 1817 a most serious epidemic caused great mortality among the Indians there; a panic seemed inevitable; and on the advice of Lieutenant Sola, a number of the sick neophytes were removed by the *padres* to the other side of the bay. The change of climate proved highly beneficial; the region of Mount Tamalpais was found singularly attractive and a decision to start a branch establishment, or *asistencia*, of the mission at San Francisco was a natural result. The patronage of San Rafael was selected in the hope that, as the name itself expresses the "healing of God," that "most glorious prince" might be induced to care "for bodies as well as souls." While considerable success attended this new venture, the condition of things at San Francisco, on the other hand, continued anything but satisfactory; and a proposal based on these two facts was presently made, that the old mission should be removed entirely from the peninsula, and refounded in a more favorable locality somewhere in the healthy and fertile country beyond San Rafael. It was thus that the name of San Francisco got attached from the outset to the new settlement at Sonoma; and when later on (the old mission being left in its place) this was made into an independent mission, the name was retained, though the dedication was transferred, appropriately enough, from St. Francis of Assisi to that other St. Francis who figures in the records as "the great apostle of the Indies."

Such is the simpler explanation of the way in which the last two missions came to be established. It has, however, been suggested that, while all this may be true as far as it goes, other muses were at work of a subtler character than those specified, and that these causes were involved in the development of political affairs. It has, however, been noted that, though the threatened encroachments of the Russians had been one of the chief reasons for this Spanish occupation of Alta California, there had hitherto been no attempt to meet their possible advances in the very regions where they were most to be expected—that is, in the country north of San Francisco. In course of time, however, always with the ostensible purpose of hunting the seal and the otter, the Russians were found to be creeping further and further south; and at length, under instructions from St. Petersburg, they took possession of the region of Bodega Bay, establishing there a trading post o their Fur Company, and a strong military station which they called Fort Ross. As this settlement was on the coast, and only sixty-five miles, as the crow flies, from San Francisco, will be seen that the Spanish authorities had some genuine cause for alarm. And the mission movement north of San Francisco is considered by some writers to have been initiated, less from spiritual motives, than from the dread of continued Russian aggression, and the hope of raising at least a slight barrier against it. However this may be, the two missions were never employed for defensive purposes; nor is it very clear that they could have been made of much practical service in case of actual need.

# Of the Downfall of the Missions of California

Such in briefest outline, is the story of the planting of the twenty-one missions of Alta California. This story, as we have seen, brings us down to the year 1823. But by this time, as we follow the chronicles, our attention has already begun to be diverted from the forces which still made for growth and success to those which ere long were to co-operate for the complete undoing of the mission system and the ruin of all its work.

Perhaps it was in the nature of things (if one may venture here to employ a phrase too often used out of mere idleness or ignorance) that the undertaking which year by year had been carried forward with so much energy and success, should after a while come to a standstill; and the commonest observation of life will suffice to remind us that when progress ceases, retrogression is almost certain to set in. The immense zeal and unflagging enthusiasm of Junipero Serra and his immediate followers could not be transmitted by any rite or formula to the men upon whose shoulders their responsibilities came presently to rest. Men they were, of course, of widely varying characters and capabilities—some, unfortunately, altogether unworthy both morally and mentally, of their high calling; many, on the contrary, genuine embodiments of the great principles of their order—humane, benevolent, faithful in the discharge of daily duty, patient alike in labour and trial, and careful administrators of the practical affairs which lay within their charge. But without injustice it may be said of them that for the most part they possessed little of the tremendous personal force of their predecessors, and a generous endowment of such personal force was as needful now as it ever had been.

Not unless we wish to emulate Southey's learned friend, who wrote whole volumes of hypothetical history in the subjunctive mood, it is hardly necessary for present purposes to discuss the internal changes which, had the missions been left to themselves, might in the long run have brought about their decay. For as a matter of fact the missions were not left to themselves. The closing chapter of their history, to which we have now to turn, is mainly concerned, not with their spiritual management, or with their success or failure in the work, they had been given to do, but with the general movement, of political events, and the upheavals which preceded the final conquest of California by the United States.

In considering the attitude of the civil authorities towards the mission system, and their dealings with it, we must remember that the Spanish government had from the first anticipated the gradual transformation of the missions into *pueblos* and parishes, and with this, the substitution of the regular clergy for the Franciscan *padres*. This was part of the general plan of colonization, of which the mission settlements were regarded as forming only the beginning. Their work was to bring the heathen into the fold of the church, to subdue them to the conditions of civilization, to instruct them in the arts of peace, and thus to prepare them for citizenship; and this done, it was purposed that they should be straightway removed from the charge of the fathers and placed under civil jurisdiction. No decisive step towards the accomplishment of this design was, however, taken for many years; and meanwhile, the fathers jealously resisted every effort of the government to interfere with their prerogatives. At length, with little comprehension of the nature of the materials out of which citizens were thus to be manufactured, and with quite as little realization of the fact that the paternal methods of education adopted by the *padres* were calculated, not to train their neophytes to self-government, but to keep them in a state of perpetual tutelage, the Spanish Cortes decreed that all missions which had then been in existence ten years should at once be turned over to bishops, and the Indians attached to them made subject to civil authority. Though promulgated in 1813, this decree was not published in California till 1820, and even then was practically a dead letter. Two years later, California became a province of the Mexican Empire, and in due course the new government turned its attention to the missions, in 1833 ordering their complete secularization. The atrocious mishandling by both Spain and Mexico of the funds by which they had been kept up, and the large demands made later upon them for provisions and money, had by this time made serious inroads upon their resources notwithstanding which they had faithfully persisted in their work. The new law now dealt them a crushing blow. Ten years of great confusion followed, and then an effort was made to save them from the complete ruin by which they were threatened by a proclamation ordering that the more important of them, twelve in number, should be restored to the *padres*. Nothing came of this, however; the collapse continued; and in 1846, the sale of the mission buildings was decreed by the Departmental Assembly. When in the August of that year, the American flag was unfurled at Monterey, everything connected with the mission their lands, their priests, their neophytes, their management—was in a state of seemingly hopeless chaos. Finally General Kearney issued a declaration to the effect that "the missions and their property should remain under the charge of the Catholic priests... until the titles to the lands should be decided by proper authority." But of whatever temporary service this measure may have been, it was of course altogether powerless to breathe fresh life into a system already in the last stages of decay. The mission-buildings were crumbling into ruins. Their lands were neglected their converts for the most part dead or scattered. The rule of the *padres* was over. The Spanish missions in Alta California were things of the past.

In these late days of a civilization so different in all its essential elements from that which the Franciscans laboured so strenuously to establish on the Pacific Coast, we may think of the fathers as we will, and pass what judgment we see fit upon their work. But be that what it may, our hearts cannot fail to be touched and stirred by the pitiful story of those true servants of God who, in the hour of ultimate disaster, firmly refused to be separated from their flocks.

Among the ruins of San Luis Obispo, in 1842, De Mofras found the oldest Spanish priest then left in California, who, after sixty years of unremitting toil, was then reduced to such abject poverty that he was forced to sleep on a hide, drink from a horn, and feed upon strips of meat dried in the sun. Yet this faithful creature still continued to share the little he possessed with the children of the few Indians who lingered in the is about the deserted church; and when efforts were made to induce him to seek some other spot where he might find refuge and rest, his answer was that he meant to die at his post. The same writer has recorded an even more tragic case from the annals of La Soledad. Long after the settlement there had been abandoned, and when the buildings were falling to pieces, an old priest, Father Sarria, still remained to minister to the bodily and physical wants of a handful of wretched natives who yet haunted the neighborhood, and whom he absolutely refused to forsake. One Sunday morning in August, 1833, after his habit, he gathered his neophytes together in what was once the church, and began, according to his custom, the celebration of the mass. But age, suffering, and privation had by this time told fatally upon him. Hardly had he commenced the service, when his strength gave way. He stumbled upon the crumbling altar, and died, literally of starvation, in the arms of those to whom for thirty years he had given freely whatever he had to give. Surely these simple records of Christ-like devotion will live in the tender remembrance of all who revere the faith that, linked with whatever creed, manifests itself in good works, the love that spends itself in service, the quiet heroism that endures to the end.

# Of the Old Missions, and Life in Them

The California missions, though greatly varying of course in regard to size and economy, were constructed upon the same general plan, in the striking and beautiful style of architecture, roughly known as Moorish, which the fathers transplanted from Spain, but which rather seems by reason of its singular appropriateness, a native growth of the new soil. The edifices which now, whether in ruins or in restoration, still testify to the skill and energy of their pious designers, were in all cases later, in most cases much later, than the settlements themselves. At the outset, a few rude buildings of wood or adobe were deemed sufficient for the temporary accommodation of priests and converts, and the celebration of religious services. Then, little by little, substantial structures in brick or stone took the place of these, and what we now think of as the mission came into being.

The best account left us of the mission establishment in its palmy days is that given by De Mofras in his careful record of travel and exploration along the Pacific Coast; and often quoted as this has been, we still cannot do better here than to translate some portions of it anew. The observant Frenchman wrote with his eye mainly upon what was perhaps the most completely typical of all the missions—that of San Luis Rey. But his description, though containing a number of merely local particulars, was intended to be general and for this reason may the more properly be reproduced in this place.

"The edifice," he wrote, "is quadrilateral, and about one hundred and fifty metres long in front The church occupies one of the wings. The facade is ornamented with a gallery [or arcade]. The building, a single storey in height, is generally raised some feet above the ground. The interior forms a court, adorned with flowers and planted with trees. Opening on the gallery which runs round it are the rooms of the monks, major-domos, and travelers, as well as the workshops, schoolrooms, and storehouses. Hospitals for men and women are situated in the quietest parts of the mission, where also are placed the schoolrooms. The young Indian girls occupy apartments called the monastery *(el moujerio)*, and they themselves are styled nuns *(las moujas)*. . . Placed under the care of trustworthy Indian women, they are there taught to spin wool, flax, and cotton, and do no leave their seclusion till they are old enough to be married. The Indian children attend the same school as the children of the white colonists. A certain number of them, chosen from those who exhibit most intelligence, are taught music—plain-chant, violin, flute, horn, violincello, and other instruments. Those who distinguish themselves in the carpenter's shop, at the forge, or in the field, are termed *alcaldes*, or chiefs, and given charge of a band of workmen. The management of each mission is composed of two monks; the elder looks after internal administration and religious instruction; the younger has direction of agricultural work. . . For the sake of order and morals, whites are employed only where strictly necessary, for the fathers know their influence to be altogether harmful, and that they lead the Indians to gambling and drunkenness, to which vices they are already too prone. To encourage the natives in their tasks, the fathers themselves often lend a hand, and everywhere furnish an example of industry. Necessity has made them industrious. One is struck with astonishment on observing that, with such meagre resources, often without European workmen or any skilled help, but with the assistance only of savages, always unintelligent and often hostile, they have yet succeeded in executing such works of architecture and engineering as mills, machinery, bridges, roads, and canals for irrigation. For the erection of nearly all the mission buildings it was necessary to bring to the sites chosen, beams cut on mountains eight or ten leagues away, and to teach the Indians to burn lime, cut stone, and make bricks.

"Around the mission," De Mofras continues, "are the huts of the neophytes, and the dwellings of some white colonists. Besides the central establishment, there exists, for a space of thirty or forty leagues, accessory farms to the number of fifteen or twenty, and branch chapels *(chapelles succursales)*. Opposite the mission is a guard-house for an escort, composed of four cavalry soldiers and a sergeant. These act as messengers, carrying orders from one mission to another, and in the earlier days of conquest repelled the savages who would sometimes attack the settlement."

Of the daily life and routine of a mission, accounts of travellers enable us to form a pretty vivid picture; and though doubtless changes of detail might be marked in passing from place to place, the larger and more essential features would be found common to all the establishments.

At sunrise the little community was already astir, and then the *Angelus* summoned all to the church, where mass .was said, and a short time given to the religious instruction of the neophytes. Breakfast followed, composed mainly of the staple dish *atole*, or pottage of roasted barley. This finished, the

Indians repaired in squads, each under the supervision of its *alcalde*, to their various tasks in workshop and field. Between eleven and twelve o'clock, a wholesome and sufficiently generous midday meal was served out. At two, work was resumed. An hour or so before sunset, the bell again tolled for the *Angelus;* evening mass was performed; and after supper had been eaten, the day closed with dance, or music, or some simple games of chance. Thus week by week, and month by month, with monotonous regularity, life ran its unbroken course; and what with the labours directly connected with the management of the mission itself, the tending of sheep and cattle in the neighboring ranches, and the care of the gardens and orchards upon which the population was largely dependent for subsistence, there was plenty to occupy the attention of the *padres*, and quite enough work to be done by the Indians under their charge. But all this does not exhaust the list of mission activities. For in course of time, as existence became more settled, and the children of the early converts shot up into boys and girls, various industries were added to such first necessary occupations, and the natives were taught to work at the forge and the bench, to make saddles and shoes, to weave, and cut, and sew. In these and similar acts, many of them acquired considerable proficiency.

It is pleasant enough to look back upon such a busy yet placid life. But while we may justly acknowledge its antique, pastoral charm, we must guard ourselves against the temptation to idealization. Beautiful in many respects it must have been; but its shadows were long and deep. According to the first principles adopted by the missionaries, the domesticated Indians were held down rigorously in a condition of servile dependence and subjection. They were indeed, as one of the early travellers in California put it, slaves under another name—slaves to the cast-iron power of a system which, like all systems, was capable of unlimited abuse, and which, at the very best, was narrow and arbitrary. Every vestige of freedom was taken from them when they entered, or were brought into, the settlement. Henceforth they belonged, body and soul, to the mission and its authority. Their tasks were assigned to them, their movements controlled, the details of their daily doings dictated, by those who were to all intents and purposes their absolute masters; and corporal punishment was visited freely not only upon those who were guilty of actual misdemeanor, but also upon such as failed in attendance at church, or, when there, did not conduct themselves properly. From time to time some unusually turbulent spirit would rise against such paternal despotism, and break away to his old savage life. But these cases, we are told, were of rare occurrence. The California Indians were for the most part indolent, apathetic, and of low intelligence; and as, under domestication, they were clothed, housed and fed, while the labour demanded from them was rarely excessive, they were wont as a rule to accept the change from the hardships of their former rough existence to the comparative comfort of the mission, if not exactly in a spirit of gratitude, at any rate with a certain brutal contentment.

# Of the Mission System and its Results

It does not fall within the scope of this little sketch, in which nothing more has been aimed at than to tell an interesting story in the simplest possible way, to enter into any discussion of a question to which what has just been said might naturally seem to ea the question, namely, of the results, immediate and remote, of the mission system in California. The widely divergent conclusions on this subject registered by the historians will, on investigation, be found, as in most such cases, to depend quite as much upon bias of mind and preconceived ideals, as upon the bare facts presented, concerning which, one would imagine, there can hardly be much difference of opinion. To decide upon the value of a given social experiment, we must, to begin with, make up our minds as to what we should wish to see achieved; and where there is no unanimity concerning the object to be reached, there will scarcely be any in respect of the means employed. It is not to be wondered at, therefore, that critical judgment upon the Franciscan missionaries and their work has been given here in terms of unqualified laudation, and there in the form of severest disapproval, and that everyone who touches the topic afresh is expected to take sides.

In their favor it must, I think, be universally admitted that they wrought always with the highest motives and the noblest intentions, and that their labours were really fruitful of much good among the native tribes. On the other hand, when regarded from the standpoint of secular progress, it seems equally certain that their work was sadly hampered by narrowness of outlook and understanding, and an utter want of appreciation of the demands and conditions of the modern world. Thus while we give them the fullest credit for all that they accomplished by their teachings and example, we have still frankly to acknowledge their failure in the most important and most difficult part of their undertaking—in the task of transforming many thousands of ignorant and degraded savages into self-respecting men and women, fit for the duties and responsibilities of civilization. Yet to put it in this way is to show sharply enough that such failure is not hastily to be set down to their discredit. It is often said, indeed, that they went altogether the wrong way to work for the achievement of the much-desired result; and it is unquestionably true, as La Perouse long ago pointed out, that they made the fundamental, but with them inevitable mistake, of sacrificing the temporal and material welfare of the natives to the consideration of so-called "heavenly interests." Yet in common fairness we must remember the stuff with which they had to deal. The Indian was by nature a child and a slave and if, out of children and slaves they did not at once manufacture independent and law-abiding citizens, is it for us, who have not yet exhibited triumphant success in handling the same problem under far more favorable conditions, to cover them with our contempt, or dismiss them with our blame Civilization is at best a slow and painful affair, as we half-civilized people ought surely to understand by this time—a matter not of individuals and years, but of generations and centuries; and nothing permanent has ever yet been gained by any attempt, how promising soever it may have seemed, to force the natural processes of social evolution. The mission *padres* bore the cross from point to point along the far-off Pacific coast; they built churches, they founded settlements, they gave their strength to the uplifting of the heathen. Little that was enduring came out of all this toil. Perhaps this was partly because their methods were shortsighted, their means inadequate o the ends proposed. But when we remember that they had set their hands to an almost impossible task, we shall perhaps be inclined rather to acknowledge their partial success, than to deal harshly with them on the score of their manifest failure.

Be all this as it may, however, the missions of California passed away, leaving practically nothing behind them but a memory. Yet this is surely a memory to be cherished by all who feel a pious reverence for the past, and whose hearts are responsive to the sense of tears that there is in mortal things. And alike for those who live beneath the blue skies of California, and for those who wander awhile as visitors among her scenes of wonder and enchantment, the old mission buildings will ever be objects of curious and unique interest. Survivals from a by-gone era, embodiments not only of the purposes of their founders, but of the faith which built the great cathedrals of Europe, they stand pathetic figures in a world to which they do not seem to belong. In the noise and bustle of the civilization which is taking possession of what was once their territory, they have no share. The life about them looks towards the future. They point mutely to the past. A tender sentiment clings about them; in their hushed enclosures we breathe at drowsy old-world atmosphere of peace; to linger within their walls, to muse in their graveyards, is to step out of the noisy present into the silence of departed years. In a land where everything is of yesterday, and whose marvellous natural beauties are but rarely touched with the associations of history or charms of romance, these things have a subtle and peculiar power—a magic not to be resisted by any one who turns aside for an hour or two from the highways of the modern world, to dream among the scenes where the old *padres* toiled and died. And as in imagination he there calls up the ghostly figures of neophyte and soldier and priest, now busy with the day's task-work, now kneeling at twilight mass in the dimly-lighted chapel; as the murmur of strange voices and the faint music of bell and chant steal in upon his ears; he will hardly fail to realize that, however much or little the Franciscan missionaries accomplished for California, they have passed down to our prosaic after-generation a legacy of poetry, whereof the sweetness will not soon die away.

THE END.

Printed in Poland
by Amazon Fulfillment
Poland Sp. z o.o., Wrocław